Fossil hunting 101

– a guide for the absolute newbie

by

Michael Maisch

©2018 Dr. Michael W. Maisch, Wieslesweg 7, D-72461 Albstadt-Tailfingen, Germany

1st Edition

All rights reserved. No portion of this book may be reproduced in any form without permission from the publisher, except as permitted by U.S. copyright law. For permissions contact: maisch@uni-tuebingen.de

ISBN 9781980415558

Foreword

I am afraid there is not much to see here, dear reader. Forewords are usually boring as hell.

I wrote this book because I think that really useful and reasonably prized guides for aspiring fossil hunters that have absolutely no idea how to start their new hobby are lacking. I also wrote it out of the sheer fun of it. Originally I wanted to include pretentious and very technical chapters on Earth's history and the major fossil groups you may find, as well as an extensive glossary. I skipped that. I consider it a bit unnecessary in our modern times when you can google everything within a blink of an eye from anywhere in the world. Instead I wanted to put together some real practical advice, based on my own, almost life-long experience as a fossil collector, my long experience as a professional paleontologist and my somewhat shorter experience as a fossil dealer.

We outdoor paleontologists, and particularly those who do it for a living by working hard, are tough guys and we do not care much about squeamishness. We call a spade a spade. You will find strong opinions on some matters, like fossil dealers, fossil protection laws and the role of scientists in here. You will not always like them, but does it really matter? They are my opinions and I do not force you to share them, you are totally entitled to keep your own. I hope the things I have to say about how to get started as a fossil hunter make up for the annoying rants thrown in here and there. Maybe you find those tirades amusing. Then you have at least not wasted your money.

Mostly, I really hope you enjoy reading, and that you will find one or two things that help you on your way to become a good fossil hunter. If that's the case, I have done my job. You can't ask for much more, I guess.

1. Why to collect fossils?

If you have bought this book I assume that you are interested in fossils and that I do not have to provide lengthy and boring explanations why this is an interesting hobby worth of your limited spare time.

First of all I have to warn you, though. If you do not like to go outside, to walk long distances, sometimes with a heavy rucksack on your back, if you are too sensitive to endure small injuries from time to time, if you have a phobia of creatures like spiders, insects, scorpions or snakes many of which you will meet – depending on where you live – during your fossil hunting tours, if you mind getting real dirty from time to time, then better stop reading here.

Fossil hunting is not for everyone. It is for people who enjoy nature and who do not mind getting their hands dirty and get a little scratch here or there occasionally. Fossil collecting is a different thing, as you can buy a lot of nice specimens for little money and build up a good collection without ever going out to the field. At least if your budget allows. But that is different story, we are concerned with the real thing here.

Fig. 1. A fossil hunter's dream comes true. Beautiful golden ammonites in black shale just waiting to be picked up in a Lower Jurassic quarry of southern Germany. Ok, I admit I arranged them a bit. But trust me, they were found only some meters apart.

So why go out fossil hunting? I like to mention just three things that I always considered as the most important and most satisfying aspects of fossil hunting.

First, you get outside and enjoy nature. And you do some exercise. After a good day of fossil hunting you may feel some muscles aching you never knew existed in your body.

Second it keeps your brain busy. If you really get into it, you will learn a lot of things, about rocks, about fossils, and in this way also about the landscape that surrounds you and the animals and plants that are still living on planet Earth. You probably have no idea what a brachiopod or a crinoid is. Don't worry, after spending a year as a fossil collector you will. Your neighbours and relatives will sure be impressed by your incredible knowledge about outlandish critters they never dreamed of and which existed in ancient times. And many of them, including crinoids and brachiopods, are still around today!

Third, you will always have the chance to find something really great. Either a very valuable fossil – some of them have been sold for millions! – or a fossil new to science. Maybe in the end you get a new species named after you.

You think this is impossible? It is not. There are literally billions of fossils still waiting to be discovered all around the globe, and none of them have yet been studied by scientists. And there are only a few thousand scientists worldwide who are paid to do their science thing on them. A huge amount of the most important and sensational fossil finds ever have been made by amateur collectors, not by professionals. It is like a true treasure hunting game for grown ups – and, of course, for children as well.

First and foremost, however, it is unadulterated fun. And I guess that is what a hobby should be all about.

Fig. 2. The author in a quarry of his beloved Lower Jurassic black shales in southern Germany, where a lot of beautiful fossils can be found. Looks like the guy has fun. And yes, those rubber boots got steel toe caps.

2. Some boring terminology

Okay, I like to do this as brief as possible, but you can't avoid to learn some stuff when starting a new pastime.

So what exactly is a fossil? It's not any kind of odd shaped rock or shiny little stone that you pick up randomly at the beach. Fossils are the remains of ancient creatures, that lived and died on this planet eons ago. A rabbit skeleton that has been lying around for ten years in grandpa's garden is not a fossil. True fossils have to be at least ten thousand years old or they don't count. Anything younger belongs to the realms of prehistory and archaeology.

Fossils come in all sizes and shapes. There are so-called microfossils that are invisible – or almost so – to the naked eye. Remains of ancient plankton from the oceans of long ago. Or plant pollen from forests where mastodons walked. I personally consider them quite boring (the microfossils, not the mastodons). They do not make nice display specimens and you can not take them into your hand. But there is a lot of scientists who freak out about those things.
Anything that is large enough to easily see it with the naked eye is a macrofossil. Macrofossils are good. That is

the stuff you will be looking for as a fossil hunter. As with many things, bigger is not always better. Many smaller fossils are much more nicely preserved than the big ones.

Then there are body fossils and trace fossils. The distinction is easy. A skeleton of a *Tyrannosaurus rex* is a body fossil, as part of the animal's body, in that case its bones and teeth, have been preserved.

Fig. 3. A typical fossil specimen. An assemblage of small marine mussels from nearshore sediments of the Lower Jurassic of Italy. The little guys have been transported after death, so only one half of the shell is preserved in all of them.

If a *T. rex* waddled along a river bank 65 million years ago and left his footprints, later to fossilize, this is a trace fossil. It was usually produced by the animal when it was still alive. This is fascinating. At least in the case of a *T. rex* footprint. Most other trace fossils are, to me, no less boring than the microfossils. A worm burrow? Who collects something like that? So, as a fossil hunter, you will sure first and foremost go for the body fossils.

Some trace fossils are peculiar and hold some odd fascination. Like coprolites. This is actually ancient poop. We know it from dinosaurs and a lot of other beasts. I can actually imagine someone collecting that stuff, just out of how weird it is.

There are much more definitions, but I promised not to bore you too much. Oh yeah, I used the word "to fossilize". What does it mean? It simply means a dead animal or plant, or parts of it, turning into a fossil. People usually think that in some magical way the ancient creatures become "petrified". That, very often, is not the case. Fossil bones and teeth for example are usually preserved more or less in the original phosphatic substance (a mineral called apatite).

Fig. 4. Cross-section through a dinosaur bone from the Upper Jurassic Morrison Formation of Wyoming. You see the inner structure of the bone very well, including the canals were little vessels supplied blood to the living bone tissue. Such a fossil is preserved in original substance. Only its pores and inner hollows are filled with sediment and minerals.

Sometimes they are so well preserved that when you cut them and polish them and look at them through a microscope, you can see the finest details of the inner structure, like the cores of the bone cells. Yes, bones are living tissue. They are made up of cells, just like the rest of our body.

Fig. 5. Example of a "steinkern" specimen. A large marine snail from the Upper Jurassic of Spain. The original shell has dissolved and the inner hollows have been filled with sediment, producing a high-fidelity natural cast. This critter is truly "petrified".

It can also happen that the original plant or animal remains decay completely, leaving a hollow space in the rock that is filled later on with some minerals. Like fool's gold (a mineral also called pyrite), which is all nice and shiny but at the same time the bane of every fossil collector, as it tends to disintegrate over time when exposed to air.

Or it can happen that the inner hollows of for example the shell of a snail, are filled with mud that petrifies, the shell later dissolving away. This leaves us with a high-fidelity cast of the shell. We call something like this a "steinkern", even in English. Actually this is a word from German, my native language, which means "core made of rock".

So fossils can come in all kinds of preservations, but they are not all "petrified".

So how does fossilization work? To put it plain and simple, the first requirement for it usually is an ancient tragedy. Some critter dies. The carcass ideally is washed into a river or lake, or an ocean, and sinks to the lake bottom or sea floor, well… down to the ground, whatever it's called. If it is covered fast enough by mud, sand or something like that, it has good chances to get preserved. Layer upon layer of stuff accumulates above the poor deceased creature.

We call that stuff which sinks down to the bottom of an ocean or lake floor sediment. It usually consists of sand, fine mud particles, and the remains of the dead, like tiny little plankton shells. Remember the microfossils? Some rocks, like the British Chalk, seen so spectacularly at the famous white cliffs of Dover, are almost completely formed by them! Billions upon billions. I said they were boring, but this is actually amazing.

So fossilization requires sedimentation. The sediment, over thousands, sometimes millions of years, hardens. The water it originally contains is squeezed out by the overburden of so many layers, and this reduces the pore space between individual particles of the sediment. Minerals start to grow and connect those individual particles of which the sediment is made. We call this diagenesis. It is just a very scholarly word for slowly turning soft mud and sand into solid rock.

So this is how the fossil is preserved. Millions of years later it may be exposed again. In the weathering cliffs of desert mountains. Along a coastline or a river bank or at a road construction site that cuts deep through the pages of Earth's history. Or in a quarry.

Waiting for you to discover it!

When you do that you have become some kind of paleontologist. Paleontology is the name for the science that deals with fossils. Like many scientific words it is hard to pronounce and has its origin in the ancient Greek language. It literally means "science of the ancient beings". The word was invented by a French professor, Henri de Blainville, way back in the 19th century. He was himself a great paleontologist and zoologist. It has stuck with us ever since.

So if you become a collector you more precisely become an "amateur paleontologist". Amateur because you do it for the love of it - the word comes from the Latin word 'amare', which means 'to love' or 'to like'. Not because you are paid for it like some professor at university or some curator at the natural history museum. And of course because you do not have a Ph. D. in paleontology.

Not having a Ph. D. makes you an amateur for lifetime, regardless how much knowledge you accumulate over the years, and how great your discoveries may be. Live with it. Many people in the academic establishment will always look down at you as some kind of "second class" paleontologist. I have to know. I got a Ph. D. myself, but started as a simple fossil collector. Don't get upset. Instead be proud of who you are. Doing something just because you love to do it, like rescuing fossils from the destruction by weathering or quarry machines just because you think they are great and you like them is, in my humble opinion, much more honorable than doing it just because you get a pay check for it every month.

There are a lot of subdisciplines of paleontology. Scientists like to subdivide things, including themselves. A guy working on fossil animals is a paleozoologist, a girl working on fossil plants a paleobotanist. Someone who, for whatever reasons, studies microfossils is a micropaleontologist. Someone who studies only trace fossils is a paleoichnologist. The list goes on and on. There are more than 50 'subdisciplines' of the small science that is paleontology.

You don't need to bother. The greatest paleontologists of all time never bothered as well. They were just paleontologists, and they studied what interested them and what they liked.

Some words on evolution. Oh hell yeah, evolution. Ever since Darwin it has not been as controversially discusses as nowadays, particularly in the United States. I am a trained paleontologist and I can only tell you one thing. No sensible being can deny the fact that if you look at the layers of sediments deposited over the eons on our planet, you see a gradual, and sometimes not so gradual, change in the life forms that inhabited it.

And then comes deep time. A fossil is worth close to nothing without a proper dating. And scientists have dated a lot of stuff in the past one hundred years. And you will never find a single dinosaur bone in layers that have been dated as younger than 65 million years. Fact. So life has changed. Stuff has started simple and has grown in complexity and diversity through time, until *Homo sapiens* arrived. And it probably still does, although no scientist has ever seen a new species coming about. That pretty certainly is because the sciences of biology and palaeontology are young, only a few hundred years old, and the idea of evolution is even more recent. It should take much longer than that for a new species to emerge.

I don't want to fool you or tell you that I know everything. Nobody knows how the first living cells appeared on this planet. It is one of the great mysteries of science how life came about. Maybe it was just by chance, maybe it was intelligent design, maybe it was God's creation. I cannot decide this question, I have not been around 4 billion years ago. And no scientist so far provided a really convincing and universally accepted explanation how something as complex as the first living organism appeared just by the random combination of some organic molecules.

But evolution nonetheless is the best hypothesis we have at hand so far for explaining what we see in the fossil documents of Earth's history. How this evolution worked, whether it was just a random process of mutation, selection and genetic drift, as the neodarwinian paradigm has it, whether there were intelligent beings involved at times who gave life on Earth a kick in the right direction every couple of millions of years, or whether it is all the plan of a creator God unfolding we actually do not know. But that evolution took place, that there were no fish in the Precambrian oceans more than 500 million years ago, that there were no dinosaurs in the coal swamps of the Carboniferous more than 300 million years ago, and that there were no humans in the Jurassic 150 million years ago is a scientific fact.

Palaeontologists study evolution. It does not mean that they are atheists. Some of the most famous palaeontologists of the past and present were devout Christians. Whether it is Friedrich von Huene, the great German dinosaur hunter who described more new dinosaur species than any other European researcher ever, or whether it is Simon Conway Morris, professor at the prestigious Cambridge University in the UK, who has studied some of the most bizarre and most fascinating early fossils and has won innumerable awards for his admirable research.

So do not think that collecting fossils and your personal religious beliefs do not fit together. They fit for these outstanding professors of the past and present. What is sufficient for them should be twice sufficient for you.

Deep time is another thing. You can talk about evolution and how it works with a couple of beers all night long, and that is fine and makes you an intelligent and likeable person. To deny deep time and to insist that the Earth is only 6000 years old makes you a complete doofus. The dating of rocks is not based on some vague interpretation of usually ill-preserved and incomplete fossils, as so many things in paleontology unfortunately but necessarily are. It is based on natural laws, and as Scotty more than once said in Star Trek: "Ya cannae change the laws of physics".

The Earth is ancient. More ancient than any human being can ever grasp, more than four billion years, and most of the time that it existed, there was life on this planet, and it has left its fossil traces in the rocks. Apart from going into outer space, to venture into the abysses of deep time is probably the most exceptional intellectual adventure a human being can have, so hop on board and start fossil hunting. Lecture is over, we can now get to some practical tips and tricks. But first…

3. An unwanted and irritating autobiographical interlude

You may ask yourself why you should believe me any of the tips and tricks that we will get to just in a couple of minutes. Oh yeah, I told you I got a Ph. D. in paleontology and you may be impressed by that fact. It may be even more impressive to hear that I published almost 200 technical articles, some of them in major academic journals, and was involved in the description of around 100 new genera and species. Does this make me a good fossil hunter?

The answer simply is: no, not at all. I know a lot of colleagues in academia who are "armchair palaeontologist". They hate fieldwork. It's bad for their skin to stay outside for too long, maybe. They prefer to shuffle around old specimens in museum drawers or hide behind their computer screens. Sometimes great discoveries lie hidden in those drawers, sure, but good fossil hunters they are not. I occasionally suspect that some of them are hardly able to tell the front from the back end of a geological hammer.

You may be more inclined to believe me when I tell you that the first book I ever possessed, age three, was a dinosaur book, and that I have been collecting fossils ever since, for 42 years now. I am still in the field every week, usually several times. I have a big private collection of more than 30.000 specimens that I all found and prepared – that is freed them from the adjacent rock – myself, including some that are totally unique or of as yet undescribed species.

Fig. 6. The author in the deserts of northwestern China in 2001. Hunting dinosaurs... but mostly finding fossil turtles.

I have been hunting fossils privately, as a professional paleontologist and more recently as one of those infernal fossil dealers in many countries of Europe, in the US, in

China, Africa, the Arctic and the Middle East. I guess I know a bit on what I am talking about, and if you want to be at least as good a fossil hunter – or hopefully even a better one – I offer you my advice. I do not have too look stuff up at Wikipedia or some lousy internet forum. I write everything by heart from my own experience. That's it.

Fig. 7. The author enduring the hardships of an expedition to the Arctic of Svalbard in 2007. Yes, field paleontologists have it so tough.

4. Rocks. You have to know them!

That is right. Collecting fossils without a knowledge of geology, that is the science of rocks and everything connected to them, is a very bad idea.

Why so? Because only some rocks contain fossils. These are the sedimentary rocks. We talked about sediments and sedimentation already. When sediments are turned into rocks by diagenesis (you remember the word, I hope), they become sedimentary rocks.

Sedimentary rocks come in a lot of varieties, the most common ones are limestones, marls (a mixture of lime and clay), claystones and sandstones. But salt and gypsum also belong to them (and almost never contain fossils). These rocks were usually formed in ancient oceans, sometimes in rivers or lakes, and that is where more than 99% of the world's fossils come from. Very rarely sedimentary rocks form on dry land. In caves and rock fissures, for example, where large rainfalls followed by floods have deposited the mud that accumulated in the area around, with bones and teeth of ancient animals spread throughout. But most of the time you will dig in ancient ocean or lake and river sediments as a fossil hunter, because chances are highest to find something there.

Fig. 8. This beautiful golden Lower Jurassic Dactylioceras *ammonite is embedded in a slaty marine sediment called oil shale. It is actually a marl, a mixture of clay and lime, with a high organic content which actually makes it a source rock for crude oil.*

Fig. 9. This Orthosphinctes *ammonite from the Upper Jurassic is also embedded in a marine sediment, but this time in a bright-coloured limestone. Sedimentary rocks can look very differently, and the preservation of the fossils in them differs as well.*

Volcanic rocks like basalt are usually completely devoid of fossils. Rocks that have formed far below in the Earth's bowels, like granite, as well. Metamorphic rocks like gneiss – rocks that have changed their structure and composition during the Earth's convulsions, like the formation of the big mountain ranges such as the Alps or Rockies - are also usually not bearing any fossils.

If you live in a place like Iceland, which is almost exclusively made of volcanic rock, you will have a hard time to find fossils. But even there, it is still possible. There are some very nice spots in Iceland where you can find beautifully preserved fossil sea shells, for example. They are only a few hundred thousand to million years old, but nonetheless they are real fossils.

I know of no country in the world where no fossil has ever been found. So, regardless where you live, you can start collecting today. It may just be easier in some places than in others. Like Iceland.

So how to get a good knowledge of rocks? I cannot provide you with a textbook on geology here, that would be a totally different matter. But there are many books out there on rocks, some of them for just a few bucks. Get hold of one of them. Then start to look at every rock you find in your neighbourhood. On the facades of the houses, in the streets, in the fields. Look at ancient graveyards and their tombstones. You will get the grasp of it pretty quickly. And the only rock types that you must be able to positively identify are the fossiliferous ones, the sedimentary rocks. Visit the next natural history museum. They'll sure have a small exhibition on the local rocks where you can study some samples. Or they deserve to be closed down. Keep an eye out and learn. And get hold of a geological map.

What is a geological map? It is just like any other map, with the exception that it shows exactly what kind of rocks are found in a particular area and not much more, except the cities and villages, the lakes and rivers and streets. They usually come with some explanatory booklet. There the name, age and type of each rock formation occurring in the area of the map should be listed. And if that rock formation contains fossils, it is usually mentioned. In a good map booklet, you should even find a list with the names of the most common fossils, which will be a gigantic help in the most difficult (and most unnecessary) task you will face: giving your finds a name. These maps are not cheap. Alternatively, go to the next well-sorted library, maybe university library, get hold of a copy and take good photos with your digital camera or smartphone. Take a photocopy of the explanations. It will suffice.

If you got a map, you are the king of the hill, because even without any real knowledge you have a guideline to the spots where fossils can be found. If you are living in Europe, do not expect to go to some place where a fossiliferous formation is indicated and find dozens of beautiful specimens immediately. Usually you will find dense forests, green fields and not a single good specimen. Geological maps are, in areas with much vegetation, usually based on a large number of data. Many of them subsurface data, that means boreholes were drilled deep in the ground to reveal what rocks lie underneath. Nothing will be seen on the surface.

So what can you do? Pop up Google Earth and look for rock outcrops. With a little practice it will be easy for you to spot them. I have found a lot of nice localities that probably no other collector knows in my area just this way. I do not need a geological map for comparison, because I am a trained geologist and I know exactly what rocks are found around my home town and where to find them. But for you as a newbie the combination of both may be ideal. You can look up where rock outcrops are in Google Earth and compare them to your map and see if the rock formations identified on your computer screen are promising hunting ground in reality or not.

Next thing: go there, by foot, bicycle, bike or car, and look if you can find something. But first get your stuff together.

5. The equipment you really need

Fossil hunting needs some equipment. I have read dozens of books on the topic, and they usually included impressive lists of "must haves" for successful collecting. To check every item on this list will get you broke in no time, unless you earn 10.000 dollars every month.

Most of these lists are rather ridiculous. I tell you what I take with me when I go to the field to do some casual collecting here in the Jurassic rocks of the Swabian Alb where I live. If you don't think that is a good equipment, you may be convinced by the fact that I managed to collect more than 2000 beautifully preserved ammonites (fossil squid with a snail-like coiled shell, typical dinosaur-era fossils) in the last two years only. And many, many other specimens.

I take good shoes with steel toe caps. You go to collect fossils. You will deal with hard rocks. Rocks roll. And sometimes move unpredictably. You don't want to get your toes squashed? Take steel toe caps. And high boots that protect your ankles. Take gloves, normal working gloves. To protect your hands. Rocks are hard and sharp-edged. They want to cut you. Don't let them.

Safety goggles (I usually don't use them because I wear glasses. Except when I am working with really, really hard and potentially dangerous stuff. This is probably stupid. So do as I say and don't do as I do).

Take a good rucksack with some space. One that feels comfortable to you. The best collecting spots are somewhere in the middle of nowhere. Fossil collecting is not for lazybones who want to drive their big ol' car right in front of the perfectly preserved dinosaur skeleton looking out of the cliff face ready to be collected. You will have to walk. A lot. And you will want to have space for the stuff you find and keep it well stored. And for water and food supply. Always take enough water with you on longer trips, even if the weather is cold. Fossil hunting is work. You will sweat. A good rucksack is your best companion.

Plastic bags. For the small fossils you will find. For the broken fossils you will find which are going to be nice specimens nonetheless when glued back together. Broken fossils are no problem. All of the big dinosaur skeletons you see mounted in the museums have been assembled from broken bits and pieces. All of them. No exception. So if you find a nice but broken fossil, put all the pieces in one bag, you will get them into nice shape later on. Throw them randomly in your rucksack and you won't be able to fix them anymore.

Something to wrap stuff up. Old newspapers are usually best. Rocks are scratchy. Throwing your fossils into your rucksack without protection from each other's scratchy surfaces may completely ruin them. Wrap each thingie up individually. Your fossils will say thank you big time by staying beautiful. Keep some boxes in your car to store your finds for the drive home. In those boxes, best put the big and heavy ones below the small and fragile ones.

A hand lens. Magnification 10x. Some fossils are small. Some of the most interesting fossils (no, not microfossils) are small, like little shark teeth or beautiful little crinoids (…again. OK, I will explain to you what a crinoid is, I promise. But later). Sometimes they are a bit hard to see when still halfway hidden by rock. A hand lens is miraculously helpful.

A hammer. A chisel is usually not even necessary (except when you are working in fine-grained and strongly layered sediments like shale or slate), but you can take one or two with you. I am lazy and shy away from the additional weight. I rather put more fossils in my rucksack than equipment I rarely use. And I have so many fossils in my collection that I do not usually mind if some specimens break while hammering them out. Often I am so lazy that I only collect the ones that have already weathered out so beautifully that you just have to pick them up. But then again, on second thought, I live in the Swabian Alb, one of the best hunting grounds for fossils worldwide. So, yeah, take a chisel with you.

The Hammer (with a capital H) is the most important thing. A fossil collector's hammer is like a cowboy's colt. He never goes outside without it. He keeps it in good shape and cares about it like an old friend. And the hammer has to be a true geological hammer, not some crappy old wooden thing from grandpa's basement. Be ready to spend between 50 and 100 bucks. You will get something that may ideally accompany you for the next twenty years, maybe even longer.

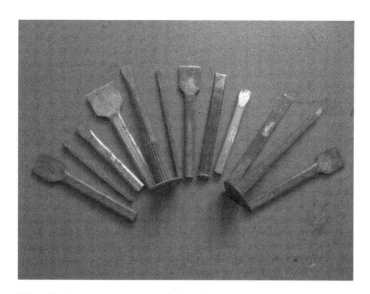

Fig. 10. An assortment of chisels. Sooner or later you will need all of them. The flat ones for slaty and shaly rocks. The small ones for preparing small fossils, the big and pointy ones if nothing else helps and you have to use brute force.

There are several companies doing great geological hammers. Estwing is the one I personally trust the most, but that is only personal preference. And no product placement. I wish Estwing would pay me for mentioning them.

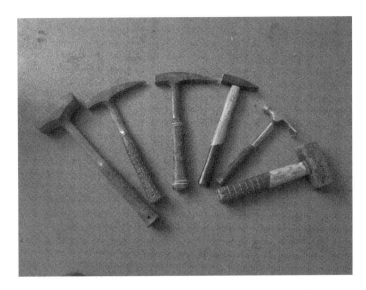

Fig. 11. Hammers come in all sizes and shapes. The million dollar question: which of these are actual geological hammers? Answer. Only the three to the left. The left one is actually a small sledgehammer, but it's Estwing made, so I guess it counts in a way. Yes the floor is dirty. As I work in my workshop. And the hammers are obviously used.

The difference between a normal hammer and a geological hammer is enormous. Once you tried one you will never go back. But the most important thing is security. A good geological hammer does not break easily, it is highest quality steel that will not send splinters in all directions when hitting a really hard rock with all your might to get out that beautiful oyster or whatever it is you have found. For your own safety, invest the money.

It will be your only major investment, because I reckon all the other things listed above are already hidden somewhere in your household anyway. And you can snatch off the expensive geological map from the library, as I told you above. There are few other hobbies that you can start with an investment of only 50 to 100 dollars I guess.

And that's it. I do not take anything more with me, except food and drink. I go out with my hammer and rucksack and some stuff to wrap up my finds and nothing more. Anything else is unnecessary as a newbie until you become more professional. Except maybe a first aid kit. As a starter you may clash with the rocks sometimes, and they usually win. Having a first aid kit with you may not be the worst idea. And of course it is always good to have company, be it family or friends. It's also good in case something happens. So always take your mobile or smartphone with you, and keep your emergency phone numbers ready if you go out alone.

Of course I have all the shiny equipment listed in the other books on fossil collecting – and more. But most of it I only use once or twice a year, and it is totally unnecessary for you in the beginning. There are two other things that are much more important and we will get to them shortly, but first I will tell you how to swing your hammer.

6. How to swing your hammer

You may be sure that you know how to do it. You are wrong. I have been to dozens of events where we carried tons of fossiliferous rock to some god forsaken little town where people who never collected before in their lives could look for fossils all day. And they – children and adults alike – just didn't know what they were doing.

Your hammer has two ends. A front end and a back end, and I trust that, unlike some of my colleagues, you can tell the two from each other. The front end is flat on one and pointed on the other side. You do not use the pointed end as a newbie. Period. You hit the rock with the flat end. If the rock is hard, like, let's say, a limestone, you hit it hard. Not half-heartedly, always troubled that you could destroy something. Fossils are mostly more robust than you think. Usually they are harder than the surrounding rock. That is the reason why so many fossils "weather out" naturally. The rock around them is destroyed by wind and rain and frost, and the fossils lie there, almost completely clean, just for you to pick them up. And you should always look for such specimens first.

But eventually you will get to the nice specimen still sticking in the rock. And you hit that rock with all your might! There usually is a narrow cleft, invisible to the eye, between fossil and surrounding rock. And you use that to your advantage. You do of course not hit the fossil directly. And before starting you observe the rock. Sedimentary rocks tend to be layered, as they have been deposited layer by layer on the ancient ocean floor or wherever they formed. You work with the layers, not against them. Never. If the fossil cracks you do not worry. It may come out in several pieces. You wrap them up, put them in a plastic bag and glue them back together at home. Never in the field. Rocks in the field are dirty. You get all the dirt and dust between the pieces of your fossil and you will never be able to fit them together nicely in the field. You take the pieces home, clean them, preferably with an old toothbrush, let them dry up and glue them afterwards. The result will be much better.

Fig. 12. Carefully collected and cleaned bits and pieces of a marine crocodile, Lower Jurassic, southern Germany. Never glue such stuff together in the field.

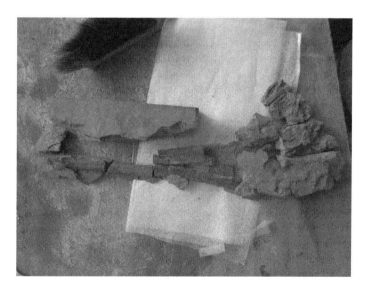

Fig. 13. Rather assemble it slowly after cleaning. The croc's head starts to take shape.

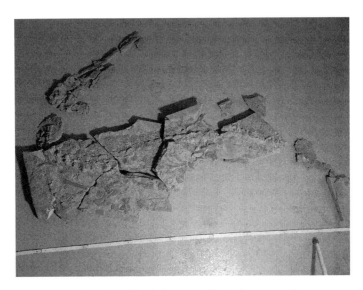

Fig. 14. *In the end 80% of the crocodile skeleton are there, assembled from more than 700 fragments in 2 weeks work. To know how to glue is one of the most important things you have to learn as a fossil hunter. You will spend almost as much time glueing as you do actual hunting.*

You may use a chisel if hammering alone does not help. You work with the chisel in the direction of the rock layers. Sometimes even sedimentary rocks show no distinct layers, they tend to be rather massive, like reef limestones or some massive sandstones. In that case a chisel is of little use.

These tips apply to almost everything except fossil bones. And fossils made up of calcite like sea urchins, crinoids and belemnites. Fossil bones in particular are brittle like there is no tomorrow, as are sea urchins and the like. They are comparable to crystal glass and should be treated as such. If you find bone in a rock you take the entire thing with you. If it is too big, you get help. Or better call the next natural history museum, for bones are usually rare and scientifically valuable anyways.

Fig. 15. Fossil bones, like this Upper Jurassic ichthyosaur tooth from southern Germany, break very easily. Don't destroy such rare finds by silly hammering.

Fig. 16. If there is anything breaking more easily than bone, then it's something like this beautiful Encrinus *crinoid all made of brittle calcite. The specimen was actually recovered out of a huge block with the aid of angle grinder. Not newbie equipment. And not a newbie find.*

7. What you need – Literature

That is right. Reading is good for you. Even though Louis Agassiz, professor at Harvard University, one of the greatest paleontologists and zoologists of all time, advised his students to "study nature, not books" you won't get far in your paleontological endeavours without some basic knowledge.

There is a lot of literature on fossils and paleontology. Most of it is very technical, and the journals in which these scientific studies are published are sometimes hard or even impossible to access for normal people. Interesting, isn't it?. These studies are paid with your tax money, but you are not allowed to look at them because of some publishers who charge you money for access. And a lot more money for a fifty year old ten page article than you have paid for this book, believe me. They also often charge the authors for even publishing their papers. And most of the real important work is done by scientists for free, like reviewing the articles and looking if everything written there is ok. A great system isn't it? If you are a publisher.

Fortunately there are many paleontology journals nowadays that are open access, and you can find a lot of things by simply surfing the web. But as I said these articles are very technical and you won't understand a lot as a newbie. But maybe they include good figures of fossils from your area that help you to give your finds a name, so they can be useful.

There are also many books on fossils in general, and dinosaurs in particular. Unless you live in a place like Montana, Alberta, Mongolia or northern China it is unlikely that you will find a lot of dinosaur bones. And, except on private land in Montana, collecting them is of course forbidden. So skip those dino dreams and dino books. Most general fossil books are also not very helpful, as they usually include fossils from all ages and countries and certainly not the ones you will find in your immediate vicinity.

Fortunately, there are also many guidebooks dealing with the geology and paleontology of certain regions. If you live in Great Britain, get hold of the three volume series published by the British Museum, called "British Palaeozoic/Mesozoic/Caenozoic fossils". It does only include a small fraction of the fossils you may theoretically find in the British isles, but it includes very good figures of many of the most common species and although a bit dated by now is a valuable resource for any starter. Many of these fossils also occur in other European countries, so it is also helpful if your are based in France or Germany. There are similar publications in most countries, and they will be helpful.

Best is if there is some kind of geological or paleontological travel guide (a rockhounding guide) for the area you live in. Such books usually contain specific information on the rocks and fossils of a particular area, and if they are any good, they will list, describe and figure the majority of common fossils you can expect to find.

But literature is not everything. I strongly suggest that you use your hobby also to get new social contacts. There are many local and national and international fossil hunter clubs all around the world. You may be inclined to join one of them. If you are not of the social type and do not look too much forwards to spending your evenings with 70 year old grandpas who will tell you over and over again how, 50 years ago, they found that one HUGE ammonite (and believe me, it is just like that), join an internet forum.

There are many online communities devoted to fossil collecting. www.thefossilforum.com is highly recommended if your English is decent. If you speak German halfway fluently, www.steinkern.de is an excellent forum where even some high-rank scientists are active and can answer all your questions. These forums help you with making contacts, with identifying your finds, with finding out about new hunting grounds and basically with becoming a better collector. Nonetheless they can not replace active reading of relevant literature. You do not want to read you better stop collecting. Today. It will not lead you anywhere.

8. What you need – Preparation equip

If you find fossils you are either very lucky and they have already weathered out nicely of the surrounding rock, so that, apart of some basic cleaning they need no further treatment. Or, more commonly, they are still partly enclosed in the surrounding rock. You need to prepare those fossils to expose all their beauty and intricate details, and often also to be able to determine, at least roughly, what it is that you have picked up on your last trip.

Preparation is simply the technical word for removing superfluous rock surrounding a fossil. The first rule: do not be overzealous with your attempts. If your techniques with your presumably simple equipment do not work, put those specimens in a drawer until you have learned more sophisticated techniques and can try again. Better to have a beautiful unprepared fossil in your collection than to throw away a once beautiful but now completely broken one.

Second rule: be patient. Rome was not built in a day, and a one foot diameter ammonite is equally not prepared in a day, at least not by a newbie. Take your time. Never get hasty. Do one thing after the other. Your fossils will be grateful.

Third rule: keep away from expensive equipment. You do not need a 800 bucks airbrasive device or a 200 bucks 'Chicago' engraving pen as a starter. Much of the basic equipment you need is found in every household.

Like, first of all: brushes. This goes from old toothbrushes for smaller fossils or details of bigger ones to real tough scrubbing brushes for getting rid of that really sticky stuff. You will of course soon find out that delicate fossils do not like to be treated like that. Some fossils may even dissolve in water. Yes, that is right, particularly small ammonites or snails or mussels with their original shell preserved in muddy sediment will just fall apart.

So when you start with the washing and shrubbing procedure always first check how your fossils react by testing it on a broken or otherwise bad and worthless specimen. If that junk fossil behaves well, you can give the same treatment to your better ones. Never start to do anything with the one prize specimen you have found. For this reason, if I visit a new locality that I have no experience with, I always deliberately collect some junk fossils just to test things out without endangering the good finds.

Fossil preparation is a science of its own. If your fossils are brushed and cleaned they usually already look much better than before. Then you can carefully start to remove the surrounding matrix. If the rock is hard, such as limestone, you can try it with hammer and chisel. And of course you use hammers and chisels of appropriate sizes. You don't use a huge sledgehammer if you want to prepare a one inch fossil. If it is a three foot fossil, sometimes a sledgehammer IS actually helpful! And do your fossil a favour and put your specimen on a sandbag or something else that is soft and flexible when hammering and chiseling around. In that way you avoid too much vibrations, which, unlike in reggae music, are mostly not good and tend to break stuff in places you just did not intend it to break, usually right across your specimen.

Always be careful to have two things. A clear working space (so remove bits and pieces of rock that you have chipped off on a regular basis. Clean things up!) and superglue. Why that? As a newbie, if you are not one of those natural talents, you will certainly break stuff. A lot. Bits and pieces of the fossil will be chipped away. They will land somewhere on your working table (or underneath it). If it is clean, chances that you find the fragment are high. If it is a dirty mess, it will probably be gone forever. You use superglue to glue the bits and pieces back on. And to stabilize the rest of the fossil as well, if it turns out to be brittle.

Fossils in softer rocks, like marls and clays, often do need little treatment after brushing and cleaning. If sediment still remains you can try to remove it with steel needles. I used to put my mother's best sewing needles in my old school dividers when I was a kid. Not to her amusement. Dividers are great. The needle is tightly fastened and you can easily alter its length. It is an almost ideal tool for your first attempts at preparing small and delicate fossils or removing rather soft sediment.

Another tool that is absolutely great if the sediment is really soft is a scalpel. You can buy them at every well-sorted pharmacy for a few bucks. Be careful with these things. They are not used in surgery to cut things open for no reason. These instruments do not belong into children's hands, and any kind of preparation work, even if you collect together with your children, is best carried out by mom and dad anyway, except maybe the brushing!

With an assortment of a few hammers and chisels of different weight and sizes, some self-made preparation needles and a scalpel you may be able to prepare the large majority of your finds satisfactorily. They will not make museum specimens, usually, but you will get an idea about what you can do and what you better avoid. How the different types of rocks behave under different treatments. When you have to be extra careful and when you can give stuff a really hard blow without risking anything.

You can not learn this from books, including this one. And you can not learn this from oldie but goldie fossil collectors. You can just learn it by doing. Do not get angry or upset, and never give up if things do not work out in the beginning. I have broken and destroyed so many fossils during my early preparation attempts, that one could possibly fill a small museum with them. And even now, after 30 years of actively doing preparation, I am far from perfect and always learn new things.

Fig. 17. An engraving pen like this is a great help for an advanced preparator. This type needs a lot of practice though and costs about 600 bucks. Not for newbies, but there may come a time...

9. How to glue in the field if you can not avoid it

A very important aspect of preparation is how to glue stuff together. It is probably the single most important step, because the majority of fossils is not perfect, they are either broken or tend to break easily when you discover them, unless they are still more or less completely enclosed in the surrounding rock.

I told you above that glueing in the field is a bad idea. So you may call me a self-contradictory scribbler. Go back and read closely. I told you that it always is a bad idea if the fossil is already into several pieces that you can pick up individually. Sometimes, however, you will face the following situation.

You find a beautiful fossil sea urchin, it is weathered free almost completely, embedded in some soft grey muddy sediment. How long have you been looking for such a prize specimen. You are overwhelmed and glad. Finally! You touch it and want to remove it carefully. It crumbles apart between your fingers at the first gentle touch.

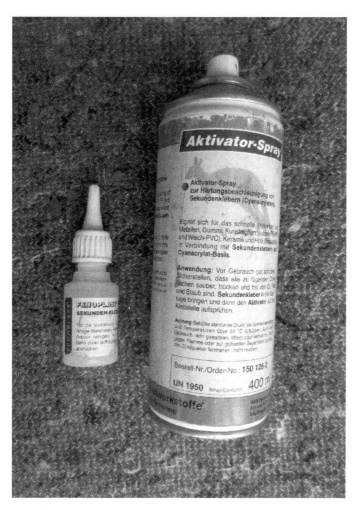

Fig. 18. Brittle and cracked fossil's best friend. The bottle of superglue (left). His best friend is the activator spray (right) which makes the superglue harden real superfast (which otherwise is not the case except when it sticks on your clothes or fingers).

Exactly this has happened to me more than once. There would have been a single possibility to save this specimen and get it home in one piece. Superglue. If I collect in rocks where fossils tend to be so brittle and delicate as the sea urchin described above, I always have a bottle of super glue ready. Or rather several. And a knife, because regardless what you do, the cap and the bottle, once you have opened it, will eventually stick together and the bottle will be blocked by dried up super glue, so that you have to cut it open again a short way below the tip. This happens ALWAYS. The best superglue is useless if nothing comes out of your bottle. Superglue and knife go together like horse and carriage.

You may loathe the idea of covering a beautiful fossil with sticky, ugly glue. You do not have to cover it. You do not pour the stuff on your sea urchin or whatever randomly. You look intensely for where the fossil is cracked, and you carefully inject the glue in those cracks. And you also carefully and patiently harden the rock around it. This will eventually keep your specimen in one piece, without completely destroying its aesthetics. There are ways to remove superglue, but usually it is not easy and often the fossil gets damaged in the process. So use it to rescue the most fragile ones. But use it with care.

And one final thing: look that you buy superglue that is highly liquid. It has to reach into the finest cracks of the rocks and the finest pores of the fossils to be effective. If you have some sticky type you will end up with a blob of glue on top of your disintegrated fossil and nothing else.

10. How to look for fossils and how to recognize them in the field

So now finally you are doing your first field trip. You have gathered information where to find something, you have all your equipment and stand face to face with the ancient rocks. Your first outcrop (geologists, palaeontologists and devoted amateurs call any kind of exposure of rock an outcrop).

So there you are, all bright-eyed and bushy-tailed. You expect to find something. You have read the explanatory booklet of the geological map. You have bought a rockhounding guide for your area. You even own a book on fossils or two, and have seen pictures of some of the things you may be able to discover on the web. Beautiful fossils, all perfectly preserved and skilfully prepared.

You walk around for 15 minutes and find nothing. Nothing at all. You start to get frustrated. The rocks look all the same, and there is nothing in there. You crack some open with your expensive geological hammer. Nothing still.

And then you see one rock. It looks different from the others. It seems like it is rusty in places. All the others are whitish or dark grey, but this one seems to contain some stuff made of iron or something similar. You inspect it closely. Some ribbed structure appears on one side. Could it be that there is an ammonite inside? The rock is big, so you take all your courage together and do as I told you. You hit it hard. Once, twice. The third time you hit it, a small crack appears between the rock and the treasure it hopefully contains. You can lift off the covering rock like a lid.

And there it is, an almost complete ammonite, only some ribs have been destroyed by your hammer blows. It may not be a killer specimen. But for you it will always be special. The first fossil you have ever found!

And why did you find it? Because you did exactly the right thing. Looking for stuff that is different. Different in colour, different in structure, different in shape from the innumerable rocks lying around. Fossils usually show all of these three features. They have different colour. They have different structure. They have different shape.

The rusty stain you saw was the product of the natural decay of a paper thin layer of fool's gold that originally covered the ammonite fossil. It has deteriorated and partially dissolved long ago. But luckily, it also provided an almost ideal interstice between rock and fossil, so that the ammonite almost prepared itself.

Fig. 19. This might be the ammonite I was talking about. An actually unprepped specimen from my collection which plopped out of the rock just as you see it here. I did not even wash it yet.

You will not always be so lucky. The next one you find does not survive your clumsy attempts at freeing it from the rock. With your final hammer blow you shatter it into dozens of pieces. Don't worry. Things will get better over time.

And that's it? That is all the advice I have? It basically is. There are some other tips and tricks though.

Walk around, do not stay in one spot and try to destroy that one huge block of rock like some Hulk or Conan wannabe. There's nothing to see in it. Look for fossils that have weathered out or can already be seen sticking out of the rock.

On the other hand do not leave a good fossil spot too soon. Fossils are often not randomly distributed in the rock. They tend to concentrate at certain places. If you have found two ammonites a few meters apart, inspect the area particularly closely. Chances are high that you will soon find number three and four. Chances are also high that 500 meters further you may find nothing at all.

Inspect the rocks closely. Try to identify which layers contain the most fossils and look for them specifically. Not all rocks are the same. Every single rock layer is a bit different, in texture, in colour, in hardness. You will get the feel for it pretty soon.

Take your time. Lighting is very essential and it changes over the day. Things look totally different in the morning, at noon, in the afternoon and in the evening. The lighting is different and shows you different things. You see more if it is a bit oblique, so the earlier and later hours are much better for fossil hunting than high noon. I usually go collecting in the afternoon or early evening. It has paid off over the years. But I also usually spend several hours outside, just to benefit from the subtle lighting changes.

Don't stare at the same rocks over and over. Try to inspect every square meter, ideally every inch of outcrop by following a zig-zag pattern with your eyes, from the bottom of the outcrop upwards and then back to the bottom. You will see much more.

Turn big rocks around if they are not too heavy. Old tree trunks as well when you are in a forest area. Sometimes beautiful small fossils accumulate below them.

Look at the foot of coastal cliffs, river banks or slopes. Fossils are heavy. Many fossils roll downhill, because they are more or less round. Brachiopods, snails, ammonites, sea urchins and many more. You will find many of them weathered out at the foot of a slope or cliff. You must be extremely lucky to find one of them directly in the rock face.

Look for patches and areas where the rock is softer if possible. Fossils weather much more easily from soft rocks than from hard rocks. Clay and marl layers are your friends. Glass-hard limestones are not. They may contain beautiful fossils, but they are much harder to recover and much more difficult to prepare, particularly when you are just starting out. Trying to get them out of the rock will be extremely frustrating. Without a lot of experience you will inevitably destroy most of them. Go for the softer rocks. Usually you will be rewarded with more specimens that are often as well preserved as those in the hard layers and much more easy to prepare. Many will not need much preparation at all.

Look at rock cross breaks, particularly fresh ones. Very often you do not see any part of the fossil on the outside, but you see it at the broken rock surface, hidden inside, again differing from the surrounding rock by colour, texture and structure.

Fig. 20. Only seen in cross-break. The crown of a big beautiful crinoid. If you want to see what it looks like after preparation, jump to the end of the book. Nothing of it was to be seen on the outside of the rock originally.

11. How to collect in a quarry

Active quarries are private property. You, as a decent person, respect that. Would you like someone to show up in your garden and dig randomly there? Sure you would freak out.

Every quarry has an owner. Some are assholes and do not allow any collecting. Respect it or risk to get reported to the police for trespassing and righteously so. I don't respect many things, but I respect private property. Even if it belongs to assholes. Many quarry owners do not care, and some are even quite friendly to collectors. I know of several good hunting grounds in Germany where once or twice a year the quarry owners invest quite a lot of work to expose the fossil bearing layers in their quarries and let collectors in for free all day.

Some quarries are run just for the fossils. These are the best. Expect to pay some bucks, but then you can look for fossils all day long without any worries. Expect to have a lot of competition, though, and expect all the good finds to be long gone or get into the hands of the guy next to you who has just cracked the ammonite jackpot while you sit there with three lousy fragments after 4 hours work.

Fig. 21. The face of this quarry in Upper Jurassic marls and limestones from southern Germany looks inviting. And, believe me, it is full of fossils. But also full of dangers.

At any rate, get the permission of the quarry owner. Usually they do not like people waddling around between their dangerous and huge machinery. So you will probably only get access on weekends, which is fine, because I assume you are decent folk who has to work throughout the week anyways to earn your money.

So if you have finally made it to the quarry, respect the following things. Always and with no exception or expect to be thrown out.

Always keep a helmet and a security vest or some other bright-coloured clothes on. Safety goggles are a plus. We talked about steel toe caps, didn't we?

Never dig big holes in the quarry floor. Never. The guys want to move their immense vehicles around there, and they do not want it too look like the Verdun battlefield.

If there are blocks of rock that have already been quarried and stapled somewhere for the next delivery, leave them alone. Even if the biggest ammonite of all times sticks out of it, do not touch them. You may talk to the quarry owner of course. Maybe you can buy this one block for a few bucks or maybe, if he is into fossils, he will give you allowance to take out the fossil, but never ruin the fruits of other people's really hard work!

Watch the quarry faces. Particularly at rainy and windy weather rocks fall or are blown over the edges. If there is blasting going on in the quarry the rock tends to get unstable. If there are overhanging rock layers – we call them "Sargdeckel" in Germany, which means "coffin lids", and I know of several cases where overhanging rock formations became literally this for unwary collectors – keep away. Better keep away in general. In every quarry there should be so many rocks just lying around that you do not need to work directly at the quarry face.

Fig. 22. Quarry face in the Lower Jurassic, southern Germany. The top portion of rocks to the right is overhanging and may fall down at the slightest touch. A true "coffin lid". Keep away from something like that.

And of course leave the machinery and equipment alone. It may be very tempting to drive around with that huge excavator. A boy's dream comes true. And look, the key is in the ignition… Resist the temptation. Never do it. You will get into serious trouble, and righteously so.

Fig. 23. *What applies to quarries also applies to road cuts or construction sites. Always ask for permission and stick to the rules. Me in Lower Jurassic claystones in southern Germany that were full of pyritized ammonites. Picture looks more dangerous than it was, the outcrop actually was not directly by the roadside.*

Otherwise, respect the individual rules and regulations each and every quarry has. The owner is the king of his quarry, and he is an absolute monarch. Consider yourself a foreign diplomat representing the Fossil Hunter Nation at a time of political uncertainty. You might be treated with cautious benevolence and distanced politeness, but also all of your actions will be watched closely.

Be cautious yourself. In that way you may enjoy many years of happy collecting in your favourite quarries. If not… I have seen a lot of quarries getting closed down for fossil hunters because of the misconduct of some stupid collectors or fossil dealers. I have seen many people being kicked out. And was involved in kicking out quite a bunch of foul apples myself. It is actually fun. So you should strive to be a good, shiny and tasty apple. Someone the quarry owner may, after some years, be inclined to drink a couple of beers with.

12. How to collect at the coast and river banks

Some countries are blessed. England is one of them. Many Englishmen, bearing current political events in mind, may not agree with this. But I don't talk about politics here (usually), I talk about fossils. And England is blessed with the greatest coastal outcrops anywhere in the world. Period. Nothing compares to them.

In Germany, we have a bit of Upper Cretaceous chalk at the coast of the Baltic Sea and that is basically it. In England you have everything. If you include Wales and Scotland, you have almost the entire Earth's history represented by highly fossiliferous rocks.

Unfortunately many coastal exposures have been overcollected. Some have been literally destroyed by greedy collectors and fossil dealers in the past, endangering even coastal stability in places. This is one of the few cases where I actually wholeheartedly applaud protection regulations. Because to me it is not about the damn fossils, it is about protecting the coast, and also the actual environment and wildlife there.

So in England you will almost always be allowed to pick up fossils at the beach, but you should better leave your hammer at home. The Brits don't like their coast to be sledgehammered, and they have good reason for that. You will find loads of stuff anyway, particularly when you get there in springtime after the heavy weather. Of course dozens of local collectors and fossil dealers will be your competition, but there should be enough for everyone.

When at the coast, watch three things closely!

First, the cliffs. As in an active quarry, probably even more so, the cliffs are unstable. The same applies to the banks of big ravines of rivers, lakes and brooks. Keep away. Look for stuff at the bottom of the cliff, there should be plenty there. Watch out and keep your ears open. If you hear even the slightest suggestion of a cracking noise near to you, run. Run for your life. Literally. I experienced near-deadly accidents by collapsing cliffs and quarry faces myself three times. I know what I am talking about and I make no joke here.

Fig. 24. Even along the shore of a small lake like this, cliffs can be quite intimidating. It's right to be intimidated. They are no joke.

The second thing to watch is the weather forecast. Rain and storm means you stay at home. Let the ammonites and ichthyosaurs disintegrate. Better than you disintegrating.

Weather can not be predicted totally reliably. What can – yep, the laws of physics again – is the tides. Watch out for the tides and study the tidal plan every day. More than one stupid and greedy collector who did not do it met his fate. The tides come in fast in places. And they can be deadly.

This is not so much of a problem along calmer coasts, like those of the Mediterranean or the Baltic Sea. Nonetheless what I said about cliffs and weather applies here as well.

And one more thing. If a sign tells you that this is a nature conservation area, where a rare species of gull is sitting on its eggs all day long, keep away. You got no business there. And of course you do not disturb the wildlife and the sensitive coastal ecosystem as well unnecessarily.

This of course does not only apply to collecting at the coast. As a fossil hunter I expect you to respect nature. Kill no animals, do not weed out plants, do not fell trees or dig gigantic holes where the bank swallows have their nests. Do not divert brooks and rivers. You think I am joking? You have no idea what greedy collectors and dealers can do, believe me.

If collecting at the coast or a river bed, some things will be nicely weathered out. A lot will be almost totally destroyed by erosion and tidal action. Don't expect to find a lot of perfect specimens so soon. The coast is harsh, also to fossils.

Fig. 25. Collecting at the coast can be a little lonesome sometimes. Expedition tent at the coast of Dickson Land, Svalbard, where loads of wonderful Triassic fossils, but not many people, are found.

It may be very beneficial to bring a sieve with you, with a mesh width of let's say 5 mm. If there is soft mud and sand around which smells of being the remains of fossiliferous rock layers, you can easily pass it through your sieve. You got water enough to do it. There are places where you can find a lot of beautiful fossils just doing this.

And, with all your collector's fever getting a grip of you, do not forget one thing. Enjoy the beauty of the scenery and the magic of nature when you are collecting at such a place.

13. How to collect together with your kids

Kids are great, but different. Kids are not adults. They are adventurous, and, if you are a parent you surely know that they just don't listen sometimes. Particularly when they are engaged in a new and interesting activity like fossil hunting. And I have never met a single kid in my life less than 10 years old that was not absolutely blown away by hunting for ancient treasures.

Kids also do not have the strength of an adult. They cannot move a sledgehammer or hundredweight blocks of rock with ease as a healthy adult male should be able to do. And they usually are not really able to assess potential threats and dangers correctly. Most adults I know are not.

So where to go with your kids? Do not go to active quarries, at least until they are school kids. It's much to dangerous. Avoid going to the coast with them unless it is a harmless place like the Mediterranean or the Baltic Sea, where almost nothing ever happens and tides are low. The tides are tricky along the Atlantic and Pacific Oceans and, as I said, the kids just don't listen.

Buy your children little helmets – bicycle helmets are just perfect – and kid-sized safety goggles. Give them kid-sized hammers and small chisels. Don't let them touch knives, pickaxes or angle grinders. Remember that I am talking about small kids here, not your 18 year old son and heir.

Go to places with them where the rocks are soft, or where they are shaly and slaty and can be easily split open with a small hammer and chisel, revealing the fossil content inside. And places where fossils are small, so that your kids can easily collect and carry them. Otherwise it will be daddy's and mommy's task. And believe me, in the beginning your kids will want to keep every little thing they find. If it is a twenty pound block with a tiny little oyster fragment inside, they will want to keep it. And they will want you to carry it. In your own interest, look for small fossils with them.

Fig. 26. So you think your kids can't hunt for fossils as well? That's part of my daughter's little collection of sponges, brachiopods, ammonites and the occasional snail and glitter stone. She is not even three years old by now.

Avoid places with steep slopes, "coffin lids" and precipices. Look for some small natural outcrops, as flat and as easy to access as possible, where they can pick up small pyritized ammonites or can find some Carboniferous ferns by splitting up small pieces of soft slate. Or find o locality where they can collect fossil shark teeth and sieve them out of soft muddy or sandy sediment. There are a lot of places like that in a lot of countries like the US, Germany, the Netherlands and England. Go there and they will be happy. Kids love shark teeth. If you are inclined, you can make a necklace with a big one for your daughter (or son, if he likes stuff like that). How cool is that, a 50 million year old killer shark's tooth that she found herself together with her daddy!

Do this and kids will be happy. Don't do it and kids will get injured or lost and you and them won't be happy at all.

14. What to do when you find something you think is too big or spectacular

It is unlikely but it may happen. People have found complete T. rex skeletons. People have found ammonites more than six feet across. What should you do when you find something like that, or suspect that you have found it?

First of all, take some photographs. Anyway, it is always a good idea to take your digital camera or your smartphone with you in the field.

Why so? Because you can photograph the rock outcrops that you visit, the different layers, the fossils which occur there. Over time you will get an archive of your own that may be more detailed than any rockhounding guide you can buy for good money. And if you document your important fossil finds in the field, you always have the memories on one hand, and the data on the other. Nothing goes above good documentation, and photos are included in that.

When you have taken your photos, inspect the thing as closely as possible. If there are broken pieces of bone lying around take some with you as samples (if the law allows, read on to learn how tricky that can be). Preferably some that look particularly odd. Particularly odd bones are the most easy to determine. Chances are high that they are skull bones or some part of the vertebrae. A rib shaft looks pretty much the same in each and every dinosaur. Based on that, any paleontologist in the world, even Bob Bakker, Phil Currie and Paul Sereno combined, may have a hard time to tell you what it is that you found.

Otherwise leave the specimen be. Chances are high that you are on federal land in the US, and that you are not supposed to collect vertebrates. Chances are even higher that just everything that is fun is forbidden when you are in Europe (see chapter 22 if you don't believe me).
Take your photos and your sample to someone at the next university or natural history museum. Hopefully you find someone who is willing and able to take a look. If you are shy and do not like to do that yourself and know some older or more experienced collectors, ask them if they like to do it for you.

That's the best advice I can give to you. These huge specimens are by far too important scientifically, let alone much too difficult to excavate and too heavy to handle for a single fossil hunter. You need an entire team and a load of equipment that may cost several tens of thousands to recover such a specimen. It just goes beyond what you can do, particularly as a newbie.

15. How to make your collection worth real money

Even if you do not have a T. rex *skeleton in your basement (there are people who have), your collection may eventually turn out to be worth real money. I have been a fossil dealer for quite a while now, and I can tell you what I would like to buy from you.*

Fossil vertebrates, like fish and reptiles, are always sought after. Dinosaur teeth and bones and big shark teeth are selling particularly well. Marine and flying reptiles are also very good stuff. The bigger and the more complete and well preserved, the better.

Mammoth teeth and sabre-tooth tiger skulls.

Ammonites, particularly large ones or beautiful ones, like golden pyritized ones or those with their pearly shell intact. If they are large AND beautiful you have a winner.

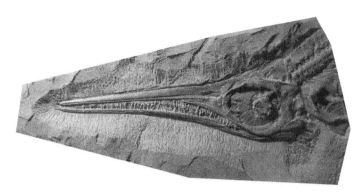

Fig. 27. This beautiful and perfect ichthyosaur skull from the Lower Jurassic of southern Germany is something every fossil dealer wants.

Trilobites, crustaceans, insects, if well preserved. Beautiful crinoids, sea urchins, starfish. Or nice plants. Plants have to make a good contrast with the surrounding rock, or they will be shelf huggers.

Most of the other fossils are anyway. Almost nobody buys fossil sponges, corals, brachiopods, graptolites, bryozoans and stuff like that. Fossil have to be beautiful and/or big to sell well.

Fig. 28. A twig of the ancient conifer Brachyphyllum *from the Upper Jurassic of southern Germany. This plant has nice contrast with the surrounding matrix. Will sell well.*

They should at least be specimens for display cabinets or the mantlepiece. Ideally they are wall paper (that is specimens in slaty rock, thin plates that you can put on your wall like a picture).

You get it. You will never get rich with your collection of the local early Cretaceous bryozoan and brachiopod fauna, although you may proudly tell anyone inclined to listen that it contains 17 species new to science. No one will buy it. One or two scientific experts in the world will lust for it, and beg you to donate it to their museum so they can write the papers and get all the fame you may be able to get by describing new species of bryozoans and brachiopods (which, actually, is not that much, but maybe it's all those experts have). If you are lucky you get mentioned in the acknowledgements of some technical paper.

If you want a collection that is worth real money, you have to be extremely lucky concerning one or two parameters of your collecting. You either are a born treasure hunter who discovers amazing stuff like no one else. Or you live in a place where spectacular and expensive fossils can be found on a regular basis, and are as lucky as to get access to the quarries and outcrops. If those two things come together, you may become a rich man. You may. You may also win the lottery, though.

Fig. 29. This Upper Jurassic sponge from southern Germany, although a rare species and of quite interesting shape, will not sell well.

Anyways, if you find such fossils yourself, and if you are able to prepare them adequately at some later point in your collecting career, you may end up with a collection that is really worth something.

If you buy expensive fossils at fossil shows to invest your money, it usually is a bad idea until it is an absolute ultra-rarity. Something like the British Guiana magenta is among stamps.

I give you a practical example to illustrate this. Let's assume a fossil dealer sells a skeleton of an ichthyosaur (I have sold many, so I know what I talk about) for 20.000. He has himself bought it from an old collection for 10.000. He had to invest a lot of time to restore the specimen and to prepare it anew, so that it looks neat, maybe two months' worth of hard work. He had to buy expensive glue and resin to harden it. Maybe the shale slab it was in was rotten and he had to take the entire skeleton out, bone by bone, and put it into a new slab which can cost up to a few hundred bucks a square meter. Then he has to get the specimen to a big fossil show, because you can not sell stuff like that on Ebay or the next flea market. If it is one like the big shows as in Tuscon, Denver, Munich or Tokyo, this may cost a few thousand more. Depending on where you are based you must also include costs for transport, customs and other fees and stuff.

In the end the dealer happily sells it for 20.000. He had an investment of additional 5000. Half of what's left is eaten away by tax and additional expenses. He has made 2.500 bucks for two months of work. This little exercise in business maths may also explain to you the reason why fossil dealers rarely get rich. They can make a living out of their hobby and passion when they are very clever, but only a select few ever made millions in that business (more on that in chapter 18).

To sum things up: now imagine you bought this ichthyosaur 20 years ago for 20.000 and want to re-sell it to me (or some other dealer) 20 years later. How much, do you think, I would pay you for it?

So yep, fossils are valuable. To get a higher prize out of your collection than the money you invested is highly difficult if you do not find decent stuff yourself and are able to prepare it adequately. It's like with the stamps. You pay 80% to full catalogue value at your local stamp dealer, but he will buy only for 20% to 40% catalogue value at maximum. And, like a fossil dealer, he will only buy the stuff that is sought after, old US stamps, British Empire stamps, German Colonies. Your "horses motif collection" and "Complete Ras-al-Khaima collection" will make him either cringe or laugh out loud. So don't try to sell your Devonian serpulid collection or your collection of crustacean coprolites and trace fossils. No one on Earth will buy it. No one.

A final word. As a collector, and not a dealer, you should collect just what you like, and never think about the money in the first place. It is your hobby, your pastime, you do it for the love of it, not for making some cheap extra bucks, understood?

When I go out in the field to collect stuff for my private collection, I am a totally different person than when I am out to collect for business. If I collect privately I take all the nice little bryozoans, brachiopods and serpulids home, wrap them up like little babies, scrub and clean them and put them all in their little tidy boxes.

When I collect for business I don't even look at them. And as you are no fossil dealer, it should be clear which of those two personalities should be yours in the first place.

16. How to do an inventory

There are three things you have to rescue when your house is on fire in the following order: your kids, your pets and your inventory. It is the heart and soul of every fossil collection and without it, it is just a pile of rocks.

What is an inventory? It is a list of the specimens you have in your collection, and it contains all the essential information.

And how do you do it? You give your specimens a number. Labels tend to get lost, misplaced, torn apart by the kids or eaten by the pets. So put the number directly on your specimen, preferably on the less well preserved side. Use a waterproof pen for that purpose. A good one, not something that leaves no mark after two years.

How you do your inventory is a matter of taste. If you do it in the classic way in the shape of a book, or in a more modern way as a Word document or Excel table on your computer does not matter much. Except that computers and their hard drives tend to crash more easily than books usually do. Therefore I keep a book. Yes, a real book, that you can take in your hands and read, as incredible as it may sound. It is also very easy to rescue when your house is on fire.

So you start with your fossil number one. Remember the first ammonite you found in chapter 10? This will be your number one, like uncle Scrooge's number one dime. And what do you write down? First, the name, if you have any, otherwise it will just be "ammonite" until you have found out. If you think it is a particular genus of ammonite, like, for example, *Perisphinctes*, but you are not sure, you put down ?*Perisphinctes* sp. The question mark indicates that the identification is questionable. The sp. stands for species, which means, you have an idea what genus it is, but you do not know what species it could be. With the particular ammonite genus *Perisphinctes* you probably will never know. Not even the experts know.

The most important information ever is the locality. Even if the name you put on the thing is completely wrong, even if you get the rock unit wrong, even if you get the finding date wrong because you were completely drunk for an entire week during your field trip with your best buddy, anything can be reconstructed later (except the finding date maybe) from as exact a description of the locality as possible. As Metallica once put it: "Nothing else matters".

An inventory that consists only of the numbers of the specimens and their exact locality is perfectly valid. Anything else is fluff more or less.

There are some anal retentive collectors that manage to fill three pages with descriptions of their specimens that are so detailed they would put a great paleontologist of old to shame. It is nice that they have the time to do that. It is sure great information. But it is not necessary.

What is the next most helpful information apart of the locality? It is the rock layer. And a simple "Jurassic" is not enough. "Lower Jurassic" is better. The name of a particular formation may be better even. The best thing is, if you take a photo of the specimen as you found it and mark the spot. If you have found it directly in the outcrop wall, mark the spot where it was sticking in. In that way your specimen will be "horizonted", that is, the exact horizon, the exact layer where it was found is known. This is rather rare, even with scientific specimens in the museums, and it will make your specimen extremely valuable scientifically.

You may add additional information to your liking. When exactly it was found. How you prepared it, what glue you used to glue it, how big it is, whether it shows any peculiarities of preservation and so on. But don't end up with the three pages description I told you about above. You will never get your inventory completed. And the book will finally be too heavy.... when your house is on fire, you know.

17. Why you should restrict your collection

Fossil collectors are like stamp collectors. At least when they start with their hobby. They just want to have everything. Let me tell you two things. First, fossil collecting is not like stamp collecting at all. First, stamps are little man-made works of art, fossils are documents of Earth's and life's true history. Second, I got nothing against stamp collecting, I have been an avid collector myself for decades. But in both fields of collecting I have learned one thing. Restrict yourself.

A child's stamp collection album will look like a random mess usually, filled with the colourful "wallpaper" stamps from exotic (and often former communist) countries in Africa and Asia, which are notoriously short of money and use their stamps to generate some revenue, rarely to put them on real letters. A newbie's fossil collection will look like a heap of rocks (unless you take my advice from the beginning). Some random fragmentary things picked up here and there. Odd shaped boulders that one thinks may be a "dinosaur egg" or a "petrified fish". Some shiny little worthless stones that just glittered a bit too much to leave them in the field. Some cheap stuff from Morocco bought at a local flea market or small mineral and gem show. There maybe the occasional valuable fossil hidden in that mess, but rarely so.

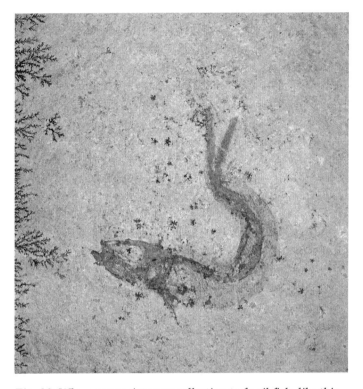

Fig. 30. Why not restrict your collection to fossil fish, like this beautiful small Leptolepides *from the Upper Jurassic of Bavaria?*

Fig. 31. A typical "starter fossil", a badly preserved Flexicalymene *trilobite from the Ordovician of Morocco. They are sold by the thousands at each mineral, gem and fossil show for a few bucks.*

There are several ways of restricting your collection. Why, you may ask. Stamps you usually have to buy, at least the older ones or the ones from foreign countries. The hobby costs a lot of money. Fossils you can just collect, it does not cost you anything except time, a few bucks for some basic equip and literature and the gas to get to the localities.

But rocks are not stamps. You can not put fossils worth a million dollars into one little album that does not take up more space than a paperback book. They are heavy. They take up your space.

Furthermore a random collection of everything is not worth much in any respect, be it financially, scientifically or for your own recreational enjoyment. A well-sorted collection is something completely different. It is valuable, if not monetarily so scientifically. With every new specimen added it becomes more so.

So how can you restrict your collecting efforts before you become a fossil pack rat?

The most natural thing would be to just collect the stuff you find around your hometown. You will do this at any rate usually, except you live in one of the few places were there are no fossils at all. If that is so, you may find a few nice and productive localities a hundred miles away in the end. Concentrate on these.

A local collection is valuable, particularly scientifically. Many big museum go for the great display specimens, the prize specimens, the stuff other museums do not have. But scientists also want to have good documentation of individual fossil localities and rock units. Unfortunately, there are far too few paleontologists in the world, and they usually have to concentrate on just a few localities where the spectacular stuff comes out, so that they can get funding for their scientific work. Therefore a lot of rock units and fossil localities have either not been looked at closely for decades, or maybe not ever been studied in detail. This is your chance for reaching the fringe of fame as a collector.

Another thing you may find to your liking is to restrict your collecting mainly to a certain time frame. Maybe, like me, you live in a place with a lot of Jurassic rocks like, let's say, southern England. Naturally most of the fossils you will find will be Jurassic in age, and probably you find them appealing. You can concentrate on Jurassic fossils, mainly from southern England or wherever you are based. You can of course occasionally go elsewhere to find fossils of the same age from, let's say France, Switzerland, Germany or Italy. Some species will be different. Preservation will be different. It will be very interesting for you to study both the similarities and differences. Or you can buy some fossils that fill the annoying gaps in your collection.

Fig. 32. Long ago I restricted my collection efforts mainly to the Jurassic of southern Germany, where gems like this beautiful Plegiocidaris *sea urchin with one of its spines still associated can be regularly found.*

A third possibility is to collect systematically, that is to concentrate on a certain group of fossil plants or animals and try to get as complete a collection as possible. This may include fossils from all countries and ages. You were fascinated by sharks ever since you have seen "Jaws"? Great. Shark teeth are among the most common vertebrate fossils and they are usually sold rather cheaply, if it is not a complete flawless six plus inch Megalodon tooth, that is. You can also find them yourself in a lot of localities. You like the fossil squid called ammonites with their beautiful spiral shells? Perfect. They are among the most common fossils in many areas. You can collect a lot yourself, and you can easily fill many gaps for very little money, at least if you do not go for the huge perfect specimens all the time.

A systematic collection is highly interesting if you are into evolution. You can follow the course of development of a certain group of animals through the eons, until, in the case of the ammonites, they went extinct 65 million years ago. In the case of the sharks you can follow them up to the present day, and include some teeth and jaws of living (and hopefully non-protected) species in your collection.

If you don't do something like that or come up with an idea of your own how to restrict your collection sensibly, you will drown in fossils sooner or later. You will never be able to get your stuff properly prepared, even less to do a decent determination and inventory. I have experienced it so many times, that an old collector with a great accumulation of fossils in his basement died and wanted to give his things to a natural history museum, or the heirs wanted to sell them, expecting the horn of plenty filled with bucks. Unfortunately, the unprepared, unlabelled, dusty crates full of fossils were mostly without any worth. I could just tell the people to throw the stuff away or sell it at the flea market or on Ebay. That is how it ends, you do not want to become one of those "fossil pack rats".

I myself have largely restricted my collection efforts to the Jurassic of southwestern Germany, because I have grown up here, I live here, and I am interested in those critters. I have also some fossils that I brought from excursions and expeditions around the world. I regard them more as souvenirs than as my actual collection. I have some from all countries and ages, which I got either as presents, or which I bought, mostly for my wife and daughter. But I always tried to restrict myself. Nonetheless I too have managed to keep some fossils totally unprepared in old shoe boxes for more than twenty years. Now almost everything is at least prepared. But I still have not properly determined or fully labelled half of my stuff.

So you see, even with reasonable restriction your hobby can soon end up as annoying work. You do not want that. Smaller is better. Less is better. Rather have some high quality fossils from a single locality, age or animal group than twenty shiny cabinets full of worthless rubbish.

18. Fossil dealers

Sometimes you may look for a particular fossil and not find it. For years. You may finally decide to descend into the abyss and visit a fossil show and buy it from one of those shady dealers everybody talks about with their hands over their mouth. The bêtes noires of paleontology.

Fossil dealers are pariahs They are held in contempt by many professional and amateur paleontologists alike. But they are also feared. They break the law. Many of them have been to jail once or twice in their lifetime. Some are rumoured to have murdered people to get hold of that one million dollar specimen.

Do I over exaggerate? Maybe a bit, but not too much. I have been a fossil dealer for more than half a decade now and I know a lot of the guys, from Germany, England, the US, Morocco, China and many other places. Some are shady. Some will rip you off. Some sell forgeries. And some have been to jail. Several times. Nonetheless they are usually extremely nice guys to have a beer and a chat with.

Fig. 33. One of the things I do for a living. Presenting beautiful Lower Jurassic fossils from Germany at the Munich Show. Almost all of them sold. Because they were no junk.

Why? Because they are like you and me. They love fossils. They could have done an easier job. Most of them are highly intelligent people with excellent geological and paleontological knowledge that would shame most of the professors at the universities. First hand knowledge coming from hard work.

They all could have been sitting on their buttocks in some bureau day in day out waiting for the pay check to come in and not having truly worked a single day in their life. Instead they go out to the field. They move rocks that weigh tons. They work with heavy machinery and dangerous equipment. They dig up huge dinosaurs. They get dirty everyday. Real dirty. They get injured. They may always be in prison with one foot, trying to escape the slings and pitfalls of the multitude of ever-increasing – and mostly rather nonsensical - "fossil protection laws". Most, like me, got children. They have a business running and they want to buy food and clothes for their three year old daughter.

So is it legitimate to buy fossils? Absolutely. Is it a good way to put up a collection? If you are a millionaire, yes. Otherwise I would not advise it. Fossil dealers, at least the big players, sell expensive specimens. You will rarely find the one little ammonite that you are missing from your favourite locality for a couple of bucks. But you will occasionally find something that appeals to you as beautiful and exotic. From a far off corner of the world where your will probably never get to. Like one of the shiny ammonites from Madagascar, where, as rumour has it, you literally risk to be shot in the head and served as "dog stew" when you mess too much with the local fossil mafia. Don't go there and try to dig unless you are a genetic crossover of Bruce Willis', Sylvester Stallone's and Arnold Schwarzenegger's movie characters. Or a real tough fossil dealer, which, in a way, amounts to the same (I am not, and have never been there).

Fossil dealers want to make money. They are businessmen. They want to get as much money for their stuff as possible. They restore specimens. They do composite specimens. They re-colour specimens. Sometimes they forge specimens. Sometimes they are forced to do it. With the legislation in China nowadays, it has become impossible for the local fossil dealers there to export true dinosaur eggs, without risking to go to jail. I have, by accident, seen a Chinese internment camp once. I don't think it is a good idea going there for a bunch of dino eggs. It is totally legal in China, however, to sell and export forged dinosaur eggs. The Chinese authorities apparently do not care whether the Westerners are duped, as long as they can keep their precious Mesozoic "preserved eggs" that are destroyed by the thousands every year by natural weathering in the country's endless deserts. The fabrications are so good, that even experts can not tell easily, without the use of expensive technical equipment, whether such an egg is the real Mc Coy or not.

If you want to buy fossils, the more you know, the better the chances you can do a bargain. Most fossil dealers are like traders in an Arabian Bazaar. They love to haggle with a good customer. The less you know the higher the chances that you are ripped off, and that the beautiful all spiny Moroccan trilobite you bought for a few hundred bucks will dissolve almost completely when you accidentally leave it on the radiator in winter time for too long.

If you are unsure, do not buy. If you know a couple of experienced collectors, ask them for advice which dealers are trustworthy. At many fossil shows, at least in Germany, scientists from the local museums and universities are usually officially represented whom you can ask whether something is the real deal or not. Fossil dealers are not held in as much contempt in Germany as in many other countries. Reason may be that some of the greatest German paleontologist were fossil dealers at least at one point in their lifetime. The country's rather chequered history has much to do with that fact.

Fossil dealers have been around for longer than paleontology as a science exists. And they have filled the big museums. What would the big American Museums look like without a Sternberg? What would the British Museum's marine reptile gallery look like without Hawkins? What would the Stuttgart State Museum be without Hauff?

We may be the bad guys, but we do good sometimes. My friend and me stumbled across a new shark from the Jurassic a couple of years ago, a huge skull, a new species. We could have easily sold it for a small fortune. Instead we gave it to the State Museum of Natural History. For free. We donated it. That is how bad we are. Keep this little anecdote in mind when you visit a fossil show. All the dogs and rats of paleontology may have had their day once. But they usually don't make a fuzz about it like some professionals do when they find half of a broken dinosaur tooth.

19. How to become more than a starter

This is the easiest question to answer. Learn and listen. Read literature, as I said several times now. Go to museums. Join a fossil club or internet forum. Establish contacts to people who know more than you. Visit talks and exhibitions or public events on paleo, there are lots of them everywhere.

In some countries like Germany it is even possible for a non-student to take individual courses at University as a so-called guest student. I had several avid collectors in my lectures when I was still teaching at university. They usually were much more eager than most of my other students, so I liked the guys very much. I guess most other scientists will feel the same way. In those ways, you can accumulate a lot of knowledge.

Of course knowledge is not all. Experience is just as important. Travel around, Look at the geology and paleontology of other areas of your country or even foreign countries. Not only for collecting purposes. Go there just to get an idea of what the Alps look like, or the Rocky Mountains. Look at museums. This of course depends on your budget, but when you go for holiday somewhere you can always keep an eye out for the rocks and what they contain. And visiting a museum with big dino skeletons is always nice. The kids will love it.

Get better in preparation. If you feel secure enough to prepare with a reasonable success rate with the simple tools I told you to use in the beginning – hammer and chisel, needle and scalpel knife – you may invest the money to get an engraving pen and a compressor (which you need to run it). If your budget is bigger or you save up for some time, you may also invest into an airbrasive device.

Of course this is a matter of available space. If you have a barn somewhere or a big basement you can easily establish a small preparation workshop there. If you live in London, Berlin or New York City in a one room apartment, this will hardly be ever possible for you and you should probably stick to collect something like shark teeth, which usually need close to no preparation at all and are also small enough to nicely store them away in the smallest of flats.

If you have managed all these three things: acquiring knowledge and contacts, getting around the block and becoming a decent preparator, you may officially consider yourself an advanced collector. At long last, you can put your diapers away.

20. How to give your fossils a name, and why it does not really matter

What's in a name? The scientific names of genera and species sound very scholarly. If you know them by heart and can pronounce something like Platysuchus multiscrobiculatus *(a marine crocodile from the Jurassic) or* Silphoictidoides ruhuhuensis *(a forerunner of mammals from the Permian of East Africa) or* Quasianosteosaurus vikinghoegdai *(a Triassic ichthyosaur that, admittedly, I named myself), you may feel like a superstar.*

You get names for your fossils by just doing what I already told you. Get books. Read literature. Go to museums to compare your specimens. Ask other collectors. Go to internet forums. Visit the next natural history museum or university and make the scientists work for their money by telling you what you have found. You may be unpleasantly surprised. Don't be too disappointed when many of them will be unable to determine even your most common finds. They are probably "experts", which means they have been paid by your tax money to spend the last 30 years of their life on working on the "Foraminifera from the Messinian event of the Miocene of northwestern Algeria" or something. They usually know all about something and next to nothing about anything else. So rather ask an old collector. They usually know more.

But names change. They are based on the opinions of scientists which fossils belong to the same species and which species belong to the same genera. And these opinions change (and not all scientists are actually very clever, regardless what they told you in school). And to make it worse, the names change the more rapidly, the less is known about the creatures, and the more people are working on them.

So they change very rapidly in dinosaurs, about which we know little, but everybody and his dog wants to study them to become "famous". They change not so fast in serpulids, a group of worms that build tubes made of calcite that fossilize very well. The fossil record of serpulids is much better than the fossil record of dinosaurs, but in all my lifetime I have only met one single paleontologist who was truly an expert on them.

And of course you will get the names wrong in the beginning. And later on as well. Even in the big museums numerous specimens, probably most of them, bear wrong labels. They have been misidentified or carry around names that have long ago fallen into disuse. Because nobody opened the drawers they have been sleeping in. For decades.

The name of a fossil, although nice to have it, is the least important information, because that is human interpretation, not fact. The locality where you found your fossil is a fact. The rock layer from which you discovered it is a fact. The day when you found it is a fact. The treatment you gave it during preparation, the glue or resin you used to stabilize it, even the stuff you coated it with to look more shiny, is a fact.

This information is the important one. The name of the fossil is just additional fluff. So if you can not manage to determine all of your finds to species (and even I do not do it usually, because the fossils are too incomplete, too ill-preserved or because I just do not care) that is nothing to worry about. A specimen with the following label:

Unknown ammonite

Fartknocker Formation, lowermost bed of the pink coloured unit

Dumbass County, 2 miles south of Hiccup Village trailer park

Found 2017-07-16

Prepared mechanically and coated with golden lacquer to make it shiny

Is worth a lot.

A label which reads.

Amaltheus margaritatus DE MONTFORT, 1808 variatio *gloriosus*

Locality unknown

Found some time around the last war by grandpa

Makes your fossil essentially worthless. You get the idea.

21. How to keep your collection in shape and display it

Keeping your collection in shape is the easiest thing on Earth. Keep your fossils clean and tidy, keep them well sorted, update your inventory. Check your pyritized or otherwise fragile or endangered fossils regularly.

If any of them shows signs of disintegration, put them in quarantine, that is, get them away from the other specimens or they will catch the pyrite disease and start disintegrating as well very soon. If you can't help the poor critters, shoot some photos of them for memories' sake and throw them out.

Throwing stuff out is actually always the best idea. You will collect a lot of fossils over the years. There will come a time when you have one hundred specimens of the same species from the same locality, of which only a dozen or so may be top notch. As long as you are not doing a scientific study on them employing statistical methods, you can get slowly rid of the foul apples. A famous French 19th century palaeontologist, Monsieur Edmond Hébert, once said that every collection needs to be thrown out of the window seven times before it gets any good. And there is much truth in that.

If the specimens are at least nice to look at and not total junk, you can sell them on Ebay, the next flea market, small mineral and fossil shows or you can give them to younger collectors who may be happy about them. If they are junk throw them away or keep some as birthday and Christmas presents for your mother-in-law.

Your space will always be limited, your collection will grow all the time. Don't let it grow above your head. Get rid of stuff. You will reach a point when your collection stops growing noticeably. Except in quality. Which is a very good thing.

Try to save space wherever you can. I put a lot of my stuff in big assorter boxes.

Fig. 34. Assorter boxes like these are a great help. They are cheap, they keep your specimens from getting dusty, and you can staple them almost endlessly.

They can handle dozens of ammonites or other palm-sized specimens with ease. And hundreds of smaller ones. Most fossils are small. And you can keep the ones from a single locality or rock layer nicely together, except for the few bigger or display specimens that you want to put somewhere else.

Fig. 35. A look in one of my many boxes. Numerous small ammonites and a couple of other stuff, all from one locality and rock layer. An entire fauna in a single box.

This also has the enormous advantage that a single label, marking the locality and rock layer where all the specimens come from is enough to preserve their complete scientific value, even if you never get around to determining each and every little sponge or snail that you picked up and number and label every individual thing.

How you display your stuff is totally up to you. I have decided to do a combination of paleontology library and fossil display at home, putting some of the larger or nicer specimens in my bookshelves.

Fig. 36. A small part of my library and a small part of my collection combined into one. It's nice to have the old fossil books together with the old fossils. Not much of a display, but I like it.

It all depends on your taste and budget. Of course you can buy costly glass cabinets with wonderful LED-lighting for your treasures. It is up to you and no one cares (except maybe your family members) as long as you do not intend to run a private museum.

22. A final word on something annoying and mostly senseless – rules, regulations and THE LAW

As a newbie you may not even consider this a problem but, believe me, unfortunately it is. And they won't care if you are a newbie! And as a scientist, fossil collector AND fossil dealer I have a strong opinion on this.

Let's assume you live in Alberta, Canada with your family. This is a famous hunting ground for Cretaceous dinosaurs, and you want to have some dinosaur bones in your collection and a great adventure for the kids at the same time. Out in the field you go, and you find some vertebrae of a horned dinosaur (they are common as dog poop there) lying around on the surface. Perfect. Pick them up, wrap them, put them in your rucksack. No need to worry. Then you think about your discovery. Where there are three or four bones there should be more, you correctly assume. You take your hammer and start digging. You find more bones and excavate them.

Stop! You have broken the law. And in the worst case they will make you pay 50.000 Canadian $ or put you in jail for one year. For picking up some old bones, you may ask? No, just for digging them up. Picking up is perfectly fine. For whatever reason the law apparently assumes that all the rare species are miraculously protected from weathering out. It is nonsensical, you see? At any rate digging is a big no-no. The professionals, the snooty academics think that it is their prerogative, and theirs alone, to dig for dinosaurs. Because they do it so much better. Usually they do, and digging for dinosaurs, as I told you before, is not a newbie's business.

On the other hand, let me tell you a little bedtime fairy story from Germany.

Once upon a time there was one of the most famous fossil localities in the world, called the Messel oil shale pit, where numerous beautifully preserved fossils from the early Tertiary had been discovered, little horses, ancient monkey, crocodiles. You name it, they have it.

It was planned to turn the old abandoned clay pit into a rubbish dump in the eighties. Due to the efforts and great discoveries of private collectors and amateurs, this never happened. Instead it is now a UNESCO world cultural heritage or something. The private collectors got their asses kicked, though. Nowadays, they are not even allowed to pick up a single fossil there!

Yes, that is right, they saved one of the ten most important fossil localities in the world from destruction due to ignorant politicians, and now the same ignorant politicians tell them to beat it.

When some big museums dig there, they usually find a lot of fish. Beautiful, complete fish. They do not need them, they got thousands of them. They are worthless scientifically, we know almost everything there is to know about those species. Since decades.

So what to do with them? Paleontology is a small science, and paleontologists are always short of money. It would be great business to sell these fish to private collectors, anybody would like to have one, myself included. That also is a big no-no. Private collectors are second class. And just imagine some of the devils incarnate, the evil fossil dealers could get their filthy little fingers on them. So the fish are destroyed. A scratch with one of the big knives they use for digging in the soft oil-shale and they are gone forever. That is how some professionals do it!

But of course this is only a fairy tale. Hush, dear little reader and sleep well…

Most of the laws "protecting" fossils are totally nonsensical. They hamper private collecting, fossil dealer's business and science all at the same time.

Many of the laws are apparently just there for chauvinistic reasons. There are a lot of third world (and other) countries obviously suffering from minority complexes they inherited from their colonial history or losing some major war or whatever. Making any export of fossils a major offence somehow in a small way apparently satisfies their need to make up for their lack of historical greatness. It may be a telling fact that the laws, although annoying, tend to be comparatively rather liberal in countries like the US, England, France or Germany. But extremely restrictive in… (insert random banana republic). And in those countries these laws of course just open the gates for all kinds of corruption to enter. The fossils are sold anyway, but now the dealers have to pay much more money to get them out of the country. To corrupted bureaucrats, not the poor little quarry worker who earns some extra money for his family by selling fossils. And this is the actual end of the story.

Back in the 19th and early 20th century it was no problem for an American paleontologist to dig stuff up in Europe and take it home, or for an European paleontologist to go somewhere in America, dig stuff up and take it home. Paleontology as a science has benefited incredibly from the free flow of fossil treasures from one country to the other. Great paleontologists used to freely exchange their surplus specimens. All the great museums in the world would be half empty, if that would not have been how things worked, and worked perfectly well, for two centuries.

The innumerable laws and regulations that have been put in place in the last decades by ignorant politicians who listened to the ceaseless yowling of some snobbish academics has ended this, probably once and for all.

What does that mean for you as a newbie? Be sure to know the law in your country. And try not to break it. That is all the advice I have. And one more thing. Come closer. Let me whisper it into your ear… If you break it, don't get caught.

You want to have a nice, fulfilling and interesting hobby, not to pay thousands of bucks or even go to jail. In the US, for example, you are usually not allowed to collect vertebrate fossils on federal land, but you may collect plant and invertebrate stuff in small quantities, preferably for "non-commercial" purposes.

The law of course is again well-intended but ridiculous. Because some vertebrates are so common at many American localities, that their bones should probably be put to proper use for phosphate production. Whereas invertebrates and plants at the same localities may be absolute rarities of high scientific value.

On private land the stuff that comes out of the ground belongs to the owner of the land in the US. If you make an agreement with the owner, the stuff you find, even if it is a complete *T. rex*, belongs to you.

That one is a good law worthy of a true democracy, I think. What is found on state land is the state's property, and that is right and just. What is found on private land is a private man's property, and that is right and just big time.

In many other countries, including most European ones, the laws and reglementations smell of sheer totalitarian regimes. Everything belongs to the state. Private collectors are made half, fossil dealers full criminals. If you find something, even if it is on your own property, you have to call the Men in Black, excuse me, the natural heritage bureaucrats or the overworked and usually disinterested scientists at the universities and museums, and they may take everything away from you without compensation. You can be glad if they do not sue you.

As if fossils were a cultural heritage. There was no culture millions of years ago. And there were no borders as well. They belong to all mankind, not to a single country or a few scientists sitting and idling along in their ivory-towers.

As if fossils in general were a resource that needs to be protected. Yes, there are some exceptional, usually small localities that should be protected in a way. And yes, not all collectors and fossil dealers are saints. There are bastards who do wrong big time and destroy more than they rescue. Nonetheless fossils weather out and are destroyed by wind and weather, frost and tides by the billions all around the globe every year. And more are destroyed in the huge cement quarries of major international corporations every year than are stored in all the big museum in the world taken together. But nobody asks about that. Because big corporations are big corporations, and they are billion dollar business.

The little fossil collecting family father in Alberta who wants to have some fun with his kids is made a criminal for digging out some lousy bones of a kind of dinosaur that is so common that the Tyrell Museum's basement maybe close to bursting with the fossil remains of those critters that will never get prepared or studied anyway. But nobody cares when 100 complete fossil reptile skeletons a week, many of them certainly representing species new to science, are turned into cement in some of the big quarries in Germany or Brazil.

In my opinion the more fossils that are saved from finally disappearing, the more that are collected, either by amateurs, fossil dealers or the handful of professionals that our overfed governments care to keep about on low salaries, the better for paleontology. This is the right way of protecting fossils from destruction, not to make fossil hunters criminals and doom the fossils to be blown to dust by the millions.

When I was in South Africa I literally kicked fossil reptile bones around, if they were not good skulls or complete skeletons. Like rats in and old basement, they were just everywhere. The handful of South African paleontologists, although mostly very busy and great people, can not deal with that overwhelming number of fossils in their huge country, and in former decades scientist from all around the world could therefore easily get there and collect for their museums. Nowadays it is forbidden to export a single fossil out of the country. It is absolutely ridiculous. They are not rare. They are not valuable. It is the apotheosis of chauvinism and shortsightedness.

It is not the fossils that need more protection. It is the collectors.

23. What to do with your collection when the inevitable happens

The last chapter may have been disturbing. But this one is probably the most unpleasant. But let's face it. We all get older. The grim reaper waits for us all.

There will come the day when you are an 80 year old grandma or grandpa. You muse over the adventures of your youth and carefully, as you are not that strong anymore, take one or the other of your favourite specimens in your hands. You don't go out to the field anymore. And you have not been well lately.

I have known a lot of old collectors who apparently assumed they would live forever and behaved that way. Their heirs were not interested in fossils at all. Glad that the old fartknocker finally crossed jordan, they hastily threw out all of his stuff, happy that now the long-planned fitness room could finally be set up in the basement he occupied so long with his odd rocks. Or they sold his beloved collection for peanuts to the next fossil dealer, for a fraction of what the stuff was actually worth.

So how to avoid your collection, something that you have assembled with love and care for a lifetime, to end like this?

First of all, write something down in your will. If you have children or relatives or good friends who are themselves interested in fossils, give your stuff to them. Everything should be fine.

If not, there are two possibilities. If you are one of those altruistic persons, donate your collection to a good natural history museum, preferably one where you have established contact to some people and know that they really care about fossils. I know of quite a few collections who were donated and ended in the dumpster nonetheless, because the overworked and underpaid scientists just did not care a rat's ass about them. So choose the museum wisely.

If you are not feeling like following in Buddha's footsteps, sell your stuff at a time that you still are healthy enough to enjoy the extra money. Try to sell it yourself on Ebay or another internet marketplace. If your specimens are really good, and not the usual rubbish, you may be amazed at the additional income you may generate that way.

If you are not in the mood to take the burden of doing this yourself, let your kids or some friends help you. Believe me, selling on Ebay is not just fun. It ends up in hard work. If they won't do it for grandpa, shame on them. But then sell it to a fossil dealer. You know best what your collection is worth, you know exactly where and when you found what, and you know what the specials and rarities are that are really worth some bucks. Don't let anyone else interfere. It is your collection. You invested many thousands of hours of hard work into it, and it is right and just that in the end you get a few thousand bucks out of it.

That's the three ways to do it. Give it to your heirs, donate it or sell it. Otherwise it will go down with a whimper and it will be like your collection never existed at all.

24. Let me take you on a field trip

Now for something completely different and less bleak. Yes, dear reader, we are through with all the lectures, the good or bad advice, the rants and bad jokes, and all the basic knowledge. So why not get out together for a little casual fossil collecting trip? I actually did one today in the afternoon. Before that, I visited a small animal park with my family and then my dear wife gave me some hours off for my hobby. She is lovely.

As I am living in a real fossil paradise I took just a short walk from my home, about 25 minutes by foot, leaving town and setting out for one of the small mountains that surround it, all made up of sometimes extremely fossil rich limestones and marlstones that were deposited in the late Jurassic, when giants like *Brontosaurus*, *Stegosaurus* and *Allosaurus* lived and huge ichthyosaurs and plesiosaurs roamed the oceans. All the sediments are marine, which means they were deposited at the ocean floor. So we can expect to find remains of ocean living creatures. They are about 150 million years old, but you have to know what to look for and where. Google Earth helped me to find the little locality I visit very often, because after every new rainfall nice fossils may have been washed out of the mostly soft and marly sediments. And it rained a lot last week.

First there is only the usual scenery you see in southern Germany when you go out hiking. Green pastures, dense forests and only a few odd rocks sticking out here and there.

Fig. 37. Beautiful to look at, but not very promising for fossil collecting. The usual scenery in the Jurassic of southern Germany.

These rocks are not the right ones. A newbie may search among them for hours without finding much. But at least he will find something. They contain fossils but they are usually not well preserved and rare. The impression of a small ammonite lies by the wayside. I don't need it and leave it for somebody else, thinking about how happy I would have been to find it when I was a kid.

Fig. 38. Nonetheless you can't escape fossils here. They lurk everywhere, like this little ammonite by the wayside.

I go further uphill, drink a bit of water as it has gotten quite hot, and I am not 20 anymore. Better take it slowly old man. Finally I arrive at the outcrop. It is directly by the side of a forest path which was extended a while ago, machines cutting into the rock face and exposing the treasures underneath.

Fig 39. That's more like it. An outcrop of Jurassic limestones and marls right along a forest path.

I look very closely, inspecting every inch of the small slope which is covered by innumerable rock fragments. There, a small, cute pyritized ammonite, can you spot it in the figure?

Fig. 40. Hidden among the rubble there is a small pyritized ammonite.

I find some more of them, slowly making my way, stopping and closely inspecting every spot where the soft marls that contain the pyritized fossils are exposed. They are rare and usually very small, only a few millimetres large. I find a beautiful ammonite almost half an inch in diameter.

Fig. 41. A somewhat bigger pyritized ammonite of the genus Streblites. *Not a bad find.*

The biggest pyritized one from that locality so far. Five minutes later a beautiful marine snail, a species I have not found here before.

Fig. 42. And this rare marine snail is even better.

Half an hour later my little plastic bag fills slowly. Small pyritized ammonites, snails, brachiopods, little sponges. An armour plate of a huge starfish is a big surprise. The second one I ever found here.

Fig. 43. Almost as good as this armour plate of the starfish Sphaeraster, *the jagged almost hexagonal thingie right in the middle of the picture.*

Those things are rare. It seems to be a good day today. I have spent almost two hours now and have collected almost 30 nice little fossils, nothing big, nothing spectacular. Sometimes I get on all fours to inspect the ground as closely as possible, not to miss the diminutive inhabitants of the Jurassic sea. I have not even used my hammer a single time so far.

In the end I decide to dig a bit. There is an abandoned forest path that cuts right through the most fossiliferous layers, in which I have discovered some beautiful sea urchins last year. I hope to find one, but I only find a single very well preserved spine. Almost ready to go home, I scratch around some more. Then it happens. A rounded shape. Sure it is just an oddly formed piece of rock. It can not possibly be the ammonite I have been searching for almost 25 years. The shape gets more suggestive the more I dig. The rock is soft, I can pull the thing out and it is what I hoped for. It is not a museum quality specimen. Not by a long shot. But it is an almost complete *Pseudhimalayites*, one of the rarest ammonites of the Upper Jurassic in my country, more than 4 inches in diameter. I almost can't believe it. I never found a complete one before. I carefully wrap the specimen up in several layers of newspaper and put it in the bottom of my rucksack. Then I turn home.

The whole trip took less than three hours and I found remains of almost 20 different species. At home I fix a noticeable crack of my ammonite with superglue. I carefully wash and brush it with an old toothbrush. It's not that well preserved, but I do not care. It is a rarity. When I look at the backside of the specimen I am struck. The complete armour of a little crab is attached to it. I do not recognize the species immediately, it has to be something rare as well. Even I have to check my literature. Two extraordinary fossils in one. I am more than happy.

Fig. 44. Jurassic catch of the day. A four inch diameter Pseudhimalayites, *a very rare ammonite.*

Did I find expensive specimens that you can sell for thousands of dollars? No. Have I found spectacular display specimens? No. Did I have three hours of sheer fun? Yes. Did I have the feeling sometimes to be somewhere in the Jurassic ocean, following the tracks and traces of creatures that disappeared from this planet eons ago. Definitely.

And that is one of the most beautiful things you can experience with your hobby. When you finally feel that connection. When you see yourself as a small part of a gigantic history, something far bigger and older than mankind. Maybe you will get the feeling as well when you start collecting. So now, go out and do it!

25. Glossary

There is no glossary as you can easily google all the terms you did not understand. I warned you in the foreword already, and in case you did not read it, you can look it up now. Except for one thing. I promised to explain what a crinoid is and I keep my promises.

The crinoids, or Class Crinoidea as it was once called when scientific classification deserved its name and was not some over-the-top cladistic junk fest, is part of the echinoderms. The crinoids are also called sea-lilies, but they are animals, not plants.

Echinoderms are critters like starfish and sea urchins. They all live in the oceans and they have been around there for eternity. They usually have a pentamerous symmetry, which means instead of being symmetrical with two more or less identical halves – a left one and a right one – as we are, they are constructed basically like a pentagram. Devilish little creatures. They have an internal skeleton, like we do, and actually they are most probably rather closely related to vertebrates, the backboned animals, of which our species, *Homo sapiens*, is a tiny little part. But their skeletons are not made of phosphatic minerals (apatite) like ours but of calcite. Usually with a lot of magnesium in it.

The crinoids are ancient, they go back to the start of higher life on this planet, the Cambrian times about 500 million years ago. And they still exist with quite a number of species, although they are not as prominent anymore as they were in eons long past. The most beautiful ones still living are found in the deep sea and in the waters of the polar regions. Most of the ancient ones that you find as fossils looked like beautiful flowers, with a "stem" and a "blossom" which was composed of the so called calyx, a kind of cup-like structure in which the essential inner organs of the actual animal were located. And a lot of tentacles that extended from that calyx. The crinoids usually are filter-feeders that live on plankton and other edible stuff they catch out of the water with their tentacles.

Most attach themselves for their entire life to the sea floor. Some can move around. Some swim. Some float. They are stunningly beautiful, both as living animals and as fossils. They are fragile and delicate and have the most complex skeletons ever developed by any living creature on Earth. The number of individual skeletal elements in some of the largest known species (which could grow almost 20 meters in length) is several millions. Yes that is right! They are the most intricately beautiful animals without backbone you can possibly find. And if you ever find a complete one as a fossil – which is an absolute rarity, as their delicate multi-element skeletons decompose extremely rapidly – you will never forget it.

Fig. 45. Detail of the crown of a large Seirocrinus *from the Lower Jurassic of southern Germany. This was the biggest and most beautiful of all crinoids ever.*

Printed in Poland
by Amazon Fulfillment
Poland Sp. z o.o., Wrocław